THE BEATLES

Helen Spence

Designed by
Philip Clucas MSIAD

Produced by
Ted Smart and David Gibbon

CRESCENT BOOKS
New York

"The Fab Four" or "The Phenomenal Four"? I think the latter is a more appropriate term to use when talking of the Beatles, of their music and of the magic which, some twenty years on, to my mind still bursts majestically forth whenever and wherever their music is played or heard.

I was never one of the privileged set to share in their day to day lives — merely the disc-jockey who, in the sixties, was lucky enough to occupy the chair of the UK's major pop programme, "Pick of the Pops". I was the dispenser of a new kind of music which, at its inception, seemed harmless and fairly simple. But this basic simplicity was so infectious as to be irresistible, no matter how much I tried to convince myself that it was just another pop record!

This simple beginning was, of course, the birth of an era in popular music, which I don't think has ever been equalled, or will ever be repeated. Having said that, I am also very aware of the enormous contribution made by that other great original, Elvis Presley. Indeed, had there been no Presley, I'm utterly convinced that there would have been no Beatles either.

The Beatles grew beyond the dimensions of the popular song. To my mind, the ever-changing facets of the sixties extended to the songwriter an open invitation to write about the experiences of day to day life; be they of social injustice, the futility of war, political motivation or whatever! Being children of this era, the Lennon-McCartney songwriting team took hold of these important issues and interpreted them in songs. These songs, though very singable, also left the lingering imprint of their lyrics on our minds, and invited us to think. As we all joined in the chorus of *All You Need Is Love*, it was somehow elevated to a level above its simple words.

As the sixties progressed and the music of the Beatles developed, not only did it encourage the younger generation to think, but I have no doubt that it also released many of us from the constraints of "middle age". We became kids again. The Beatles' magic seemed to be a prescription for "Youth For All".

I remember a couple of interviews with the boys during that time. I asked Paul once "Will we ever get this interview finished?" "We could if you weren't so thick", he retorted. But it just wasn't one of those moments when you could take offence — you could only laugh with the rest of them and feel it was almost a compliment! On another, more serious occasion I asked him if he thought that the Beatles had caused a revolution. He thought for a moment and said "I think we may have caused a revolution in the recording studios, insofar as we told engineers what we wanted in the way of sounds and ideas". Looking back at his reply now, I have the feeling that he was perhaps a little shy. He was certainly unaware as to the effect the Beatles eventually were to have on the world.

One of the private moments that hit me rather forcibly happened during a chat with George. He pulled out his guitar and started singing "I'm a dark horse, running on a dark race course". Then he suddenly stopped and looked at me! "Are you really a dark horse?" I asked, and he said "Sure, we all are — all running on dark race courses. But don't blame me...I didn't ask for it. It just happened!"

I think that the "revolution", which Paul confined merely to the recording studios, stretched far beyond the bounds of Abbey Road. John, Paul, George and Ringo, with their collective charm, cheek and talent, became more than just successful stars of popular music...more than just an "institution". They invited us to enjoy the lighter side of life, to join in and sing, and above all, I think they invited us to stop and think!

Well we did stop and think, and take stock of the situation, and the musical revolutions that filtered from the recording studios in Abbey Road over the years are firmly established as the great revolution that now engulfs us all.

...All You Need Is Love...
Altogether Now!

Alan Freeman.

The angry cry of a newborn baby was heard amid the thunder of one of the worst air raids Liverpool had seen. At 6.30 in the evening, on October 9th 1940, Julia Lennon gave birth to a son, and called him John Winston.

Julia's husband, Fred, was a seaman which meant that they saw very little of one another. Eventually they separated and John went to live with his adored Aunt Mimi, one of Julia's sisters. She and her husband George looked upon John as their son although Mimi was fairly strict with him. When her "no nonsense" attitude became too much for him, he would turn to his Uncle George who was always there with a treat of sweets, pocket money or even a visit to the pictures.

John was four years old when he went to his first school, Dovedale Primary, and within five months he had learnt to read and write. About a year later his father Fred, on shore-leave, came to Liverpool to see his son. He took John on holiday to Blackpool with him and they stayed there for several weeks during which Fred decided that he wanted to keep his son, and made plans to emigrate to New Zealand. Everything was ready for the big move when Julia turned up and announced that she wanted to take John home. The parents could not agree on a decision, and the poor little boy was told to choose between them. He had grown quite used to living with his dad, and ran to his knee – but as soon as the door had closed behind Julia, John went chasing after her, and Fred disappeared from his life.

Julia took John back to Liverpool, and before long he had moved back with Mimi and George and a childhood as near to normal as protective Mimi could give him.

By the time he was seven years old, John had started to write and illustrate his own little books of stories, jokes and cartoons. He was the intrepid leader of a gang at school, constantly proving himself by undertaking dares so brave that his contemporaries could not fail to be impressed. When John was 12, he and fellow gang member, Pete Shotton, started at Quarry Bank Grammar School. Ivan Vaughan, member of the same school gang, went to the Liverpool Institute, and a fourth, Nigel Whalley, went to Bluecoat School. Towards the end of John's first year at Quarry Bank, in June 1953, his beloved Uncle George died

of a haemorrhage.

Mimi was left to bring up a rebellious, strong-willed boy alone. He was unpopular with the schoolmasters, being one of the most disruptive members of his class, and he seemed to have no respect for authority or discipline. Now, instead of turning to George, John turned to his mother. He and Pete Shotton used to take days off school to visit her, and she never minded – they were always welcome in her warm, relaxed, laughter-filled household. She was, they felt, like someone of their own generation, and they loved her.

Towards the end of their schooldays, John and Pete discovered the thrilling, anti-establishment Teddy Boy fashion. They had their regulation school trousers taken in to resemble the drain-pipe trousers or "drainies" that were an essential part of the Teddy Boy uniform, and Julia bought John a coloured shirt. Mimi thoroughly disapproved of the Teddy Boy look, and John used to hide his most outrageous clothes from her. Then came the momentous impact of Elvis Presley, whose record, *Heartbreak Hotel*, was top of the charts in 14 countries in May 1956! John idolised this new hero and, like thousands of his contemporaries, wanted to emulate him – to be a star.

It was a totally different brand of music, however, that gave John the break he was looking for, and it came in a song called *Rock Island Line* sung by Lonnie Donegan. It was called skiffle. The sound could be created using instruments as basic as tin cans and washboards, and home-made "double basses" of broom-handles, tea chests and lengths of wire – and the possibility of forming a group was no longer a hopeless dream. John pleaded and begged for a guitar, and eventually Mimi gave in, while Julia, who could play banjo, taught John a few chords, and he spent every spare moment practising.

John Lennon and Pete Shotton set about forming a skiffle group which, as Quarry Bank boys, they named the Quarrymen. One of the early gang, Nigel Whalley, became a regular member of the group, who wore Teddy Boy clothes and slicked back and piled up their hair in true Elvis style. Ivan Vaughan, still a close friend of John's, occasionally brought very carefully selected acquaintances to meet him, as possible recruits to the Quarrymen and one day, in the summer of 1957, he introduced his schoolfriend Paul McCartney.

Before long, Paul and John had become almost inseparable, and Paul taught John many new guitar chords – although Paul's left-handed playing was sometimes difficult to follow.

That autumn, John started a course at an art college which was just a stone's throw from Paul's school, the Liverpool Institute. Towards the end of the year Paul introduced another Liverpool Institute pupil to John. His name – George Harrison. John, Paul and George formed the nucleus of the Quarrymen, around which a succession of other members revolved. By now they had advanced from tea chests and washboards and were working on a more exciting sound – rock and roll. Many groups were making this transition, and to mark their new style, they were changing their names – the Gerry Marsden Skiffle Group, for example, became Gerry and the Pace-makers. Unfortunately for the Quarrymen, their name was emblazoned all over their drum kit, so they had to stick with it!

In the winter of 1957 a new group emerged from the United States. Called the Crickets, its leader, Buddy Holly, both wrote and played his own songs. If Buddy Holly could write and play his own material, then so could Lennon and McCartney...A unique partnership was born.

DISCOGRAPHY

Singles on Parlophone Records.

Love Me Do/P.S. I Love You	Oct 62
Please Please Me/Ask Me Why	Jan 63
From Me To You/Thank You Girl	Apr 63
She Loves You/I'll Get You	Aug 63
I Want To Hold Your Hand/ This Boy	Nov 63
Can't Buy Me Love/ You Can't Do That	Mar 64
A Hard Day's Night/ The Things We Said Today	Jul 64
I Feel Fine/She's A Woman	Nov 64
Ticket To Ride/Yes It Is	Apr 65
Help!/I'm Down	Jul 65
Day Tripper/We Can Work It Out	Dec 65
Paperback Writer/Rain	Jun 66
Yellow Submarine/Eleanor Rigby	Aug 66
Penny Lane/ Strawberry Fields Forever	Jan 67
All You Need Is Love/ Baby, You're A Rich Man	Jul 67
Hello, Goodbye/ I Am The Walrus	Nov 67
Magical Mystery Tour EP*	Dec 67
Lady Madonna/That Inner Light	Mar 68

Singles on Apple Records.

Hey Jude/Revolution	Sep 68
Get Back/Don't Let Me Down	Apr 69
The Ballad Of John & Yoko/ Old Brown Shoe	Jun 69
Come Together/Something	Oct 69
Let It Be/You Know My Name	Mar 70

*Double Extended Player: Magical Mystery Tour, Your Mother Should Know, I Am The Walrus, Fool On The Hill, Flying, Blue Jay Way.

Long playing records (excluding Compilation Albums).

All songs are by the Beatles unless otherwise indicated.

Please Please Me *(Parlophone, May 1963).* I Saw Her Standing There, Misery, Ask Me Why, Please Please Me, Love Me Do, PS I Love You, Do You Want To Know A Secret?, There's A Place. *Not by the Beatles: Anna, Chains, Boys, Baby It's You, A Taste Of Honey, Twist and Shout.*

With The Beatles *(Parlophone, Dec 1963).* It Won't Be Long, All I've Got To Do, All My Loving, Don't Bother Me, Little Child, Hold Me Tight, I Wanna Be Your Man, Not A Second Time. *Not by the Beatles: Till There Was You, Please Mister Postman, Roll Over Beethoven, You Really Got A Hold On Me, Devil In Her Heart, Money.*

A Hard Day's Night *(Parlophone, July 1964).* A Hard Day's Night, I Should Have Known Better, If I Fell, I'm Happy Just To Dance With You, And I Love Her, Tell Me Why, Can't Buy Me Love, Any Time At All, I'll Cry Instead, Things We Said, When I Get Home, You Can't Do That, I'll Be Back.

Beatles For Sale *(Parlophone, Dec 1964).* No Reply, I'm A Loser, Baby's In Black, I'll Follow The Sun, Eight Days A Week, Every Little Thing, I Don't Want To Spoil The Party, What You're Doing. *Not by the Beatles: Rock And Roll Music, Honey Don't, Mr. Moonlight, Kansas City, Words Of Love, Everybody's Trying To Be My Baby.*

Help! *(Parlophone, Aug 1965).* Help!, The Night Before, You've Got To Hide Your Love Away, I Need You, Another Girl, You're Going To Lose That Girl, Ticket To Ride, It's Only Love, You Like Me Too Much, Tell Me What You See, I've Just Seen A Face, Yesterday. *Not by the Beatles: Act Naturally, Dizzy Miss Lizzy.*

Rubber Soul *(Parlophone, Dec 1965).* Drive My Car, Norwegian Wood, You Won't See Me, Nowhere Man, Think For Yourself, The Word, Michelle, What Goes On, Girl, I'm Looking Through You, In My Life, Wait, If I Needed Someone, Run For Your Life.

Revolver *(Parlophone, Sept 1966).* Taxman, Eleanor Rigby, I'm Only Sleeping, Love You To, Here, There and Everywhere, Yellow Submarine, She Said She Said, Good Day Sunshine, And Your Bird Can Sing, For No One, Dr. Robert, I Want To Tell You, Got To Get You Into My Life, Tomorrow Never Knows.

Sergeant Pepper's Lonely Hearts Club Band *(Parlophone, June 1967).* Sergeant Pepper's Lonely Hearts Club Band, With A Little Help From My Friends, Lucy In The Sky With Diamonds, Getting Better, Fixing A Hole, She's Leaving Home, Being For The Benefit Of Mr. Kite, Within You, Without You, When I'm Sixty-Four, Lovely Rita, Good Morning, Good Morning, A Day In The Life.

The Beatles (Double White) *(Apple, Nov 1968).* Back In The USSR, Dear Prudence, Glass Onion, Ob-la-di Ob-la-da, Wild Honey Pie, The Continuing Story of Bungalow Bill, While My Guitar Gently Weeps, Happiness Is A Warm Gun, Martha My Dear, I'm So Tired, Blackbird, Piggies, Rocky Raccoon, Don't Pass Me By, Why Don't We Do It In The Road, I Will, Julia, Birthday, Yer Blues, Mother Nature's Son, Everybody's Got Something To Hide Except Me And My Monkey, Sexy Sadie, Helter Skelter, Long Long Long, Revolution 1, Honey Pie, Savoy Truffle, Cry Baby Cry, Revolution 9, Goodnight.

Yellow Submarine *(Apple, Jan 1969).* Yellow Submarine, Only A Northern Song, All Together Now, Hey Bulldog, It's All Too Much, All You Need Is Love, Pepperland, Sea Of Time, Sea Of Holes, Sea of Monsters, March Of The Meanies, Pepperland Laid Waste, Yellow Submarine In Pepperland.

Abbey Road *(Apple, Oct 1969).* Come Together, Something, Maxwell's Silver Hammer, Oh! Darling, Octopus's Garden, I Want You (She's So Heavy), Here Comes The Sun, Because, You Never Give Me Your Money, Sun King, Mean Mr. Mustard, Polythene Pam, She Came In Through The Bathroom Window, Golden Slumbers, Carry That Weight, The End.

Let It Be *(Apple, May 1970).* Two Of Us, I Dig A Pony, Across The Universe, I Me Mine, Dig It, Let It Be (version two), Maggie Mae (arr), I've Got A Feeling, One After 909, The Long And Winding Road, For You Blue, Get Back (version two).

TOURS AND CONCERTS

1960 August to December: Hamburg, Germany; The Indra, the Kaiserkeller, the Top Ten.

December 27th: Litherland Town Hall, England; Welcome Home Concert.

1961 March to July: Hamburg, Germany; the Top Ten.

March 21st: Debut concert; The Cavern Club, Liverpool, England.

Summer to Winter: Regular performances at the Cavern.

1962 April to June: Hamburg, Germany; The Star Club.

June 9th: The Cavern; Welcome Home Concert.

Summer and Autumn: Northern England.

December 10th: Peterborough, England; supporting Frank Ifield.

1963 February: Tour of Britain supporting Helen Shapiro.

March to May: Tour of Britain supporting Chris Montez and Tommy Roe.

April 21st: Wembley, London; *New Musical Express* Poll Winners Concert.

May to October: Tour of Britain.

June 12th: Grafton, England; Charity Concert for the NSPCC.

August 3rd: The Cavern; Final Concert.

October 13th: Sunday Night at the London Palladium.

October 24th to 29th: Sweden.

November 4th: Prince of Wales Theatre, London; Royal Command Variety Performance.

Winter: Britain.

December 14th: Wimbledon, London; Southern Fan Club Convention.

December 21st: Bradford, England; Christmas Show.

December 22nd: Liverpool, England; Christmas Show.

December 24th to

1964 January 11th: Finsbury Park, London; Variety Show.

January 16th to February 4th: Paris, France.

February 11th and 12th: U.S.A.

April and May: Britain.

April 26th: Wembley, London;

New Musical Express Poll Winners Concert.

May 31st: Prince of Wales Theatre, London; "Pops Alive".

June 4th to August 16th: Hong Kong, Denmark, Australia, New Zealand, Sweden, Britain.

July 23rd: London Palladium; charity show, Night of 100 Stars.

August 19th to September 20th: U.S.A.

September 20th: Paramount Theatre (N.Y.). Charity Concert for Cerebral Palsy.

October 9th to November 10th: Britain.

December 24th to

1965 January 16th: Hammersmith Odeon, London; Christmas Shows, twice nightly.

April 11th: Wembley, London; *New Musical Express* Poll Winners Concert.

June 20th to July 13th: France, Italy, Spain.

August 15th to 31st: U.S.A.

December 3rd to 12th: Britain.

1966 May 1st: Wembley, London; *New Musical Express* Poll Winners Concert.

June 24th to July 4th: Germany, Japan, Philippines.

August 12th to 29th: U.S.A.

1969 January 30th: Apple Building, 3 Savile Row, London; Rooftop Concert.

LOVE ME DO

This early photograph above was taken in Hamburg, West Germany, before the Beatles had achieved world-wide fame. From left to right are Paul McCartney, George Harrison, John Lennon and Ringo Starr.

In 1962 the attention of England's youth was drawn by the release and minor success of a record called *Love Me Do,* by a band from Liverpool called the Beatles.

It all began a few years earlier when Paul McCartney joined John Lennon's group, the Quarrymen. One of Paul's schoolfriends from the Liverpool Institute, George Harrison, was introduced to John about a year later, and although he was only thirteen and considered a baby, his ability to play guitar was recognised and he was asked to join.

The group played at local dance halls and social clubs for a couple of years before breaking up. John, Paul and George soon regrouped, however, and became the Beetles at the suggestion of Stuart Sutcliffe – an art college friend John had persuaded to join. The name was inspired by Buddy Holly's "Crickets", but at John's punning instigation was changed to the Beatles.

In the late fifties the Beatles became friendly with Allan Williams, a Liverpool club owner and concert promoter. Not only did he organise various local

who all played guitar, Stu Sutcliffe who played bass, and Pete Best the drummer. On their arrival in one of the seediest parts of Hamburg they were met by their new employer, Bruno Koschmider, who conducted them to their lodgings – three squalid little rooms behind a cinema of dubious reputation.

The Beatles opened at The Indra on August 18th 1960. The surroundings were not quite what they had expected – a small, dimly lit cellar cabaret bar, with a small, unenthusiastic audience. Nevertheless, having been employed to play four hours a night and six on Saturdays and

George Harrison, Pete Best (the Beatles' drummer before Ringo joined), Paul McCartney and John Lennon are seen below in the Cavern Club in 1962. On the heavily graffiti-ed wall behind them is the legend "Gerry and the Pacemakers", another Liverpool group who also came to be managed by Brian Epstein. Their first hit, which in fact reached Number One in the UK, was a record called How Do You Do It?, *a song that the Beatles had rejected!*

appearances but, in the early sixties, the engagements in Hamburg, West Germany, which would later prove significant.

The group that, in 1960, travelled abroad for the first time in their lives, was made up of five Beatles: John Lennon, Paul McCartney and George Harrison

Sundays, that is precisely what they did. It was good experience. "Mak show boys, mak show!" shouted Bruno Koschmider, so they stamped and writhed and grimaced and played, but as much for themselves as for anyone else. Apart from these gruelling sessions, they explored

In 1963, the Beatles gave a concert in the London Palladium above in front of an audience of some 2,000 screaming teenage girls. The Beatles' squeaky-clean image right endeared them to young and old alike. Here they smile, and sign autographs at a Press reception in Miami.

Hamburg – its bars, clubs and women. Their activities did not leave much time to sleep, so they took pills to keep themselves awake.

Their employer owned a more luxurious club called the Kaiserkeller, and it was here that they were next called upon to play. This new audience was much larger and rougher – often sailors on shoreleave – and it was controlled by bouncers who doubled as waiters.

The Beatles shared the bill at the Kaiserkeller with another Liverpool group – Rory Storm and the Hurricanes. Their drummer was a small bearded youth bearing the pseudonym Ringo Starr.

Whilst in Hamburg, Stu Sutcliffe, the bass player, got engaged to a beautiful German girl called Astrid Kirchherr. She had been to art college, initially as a student of dress design, but showing a particular flair for photography, she had been taken on as a photographer's assistant. She took stunning photographs of the Beatles. She also cut Stu's hair. Gone was the Teddy-boy cockade, and in its place the embryo "Beatle-cut". At first the others teased him about his hair, but it wasn't long before all, except for Pete, had followed his example. To complete

THIS BOY

Ringo enjoys a drink in his own bar in his mock-Tudor mansion in Weybridge, Surrey left. *The bar was well equipped, with beer on tap, and even an exquisite antique till. Looking smart in evening dress* right *are George, Cynthia and John, and Ringo and Maureen.* Below: *George.* Below right: *Ringo.*

their new look the Beatles started wearing leather outfits.

In November 1960 Peter Eckhorn opened a new and exciting music club in Hamburg. He persuaded the Beatles to forsake the Kaiserkeller and play in the Top Ten, but just before their opening night, the police discovered that George Harrison was under age and ordered him to leave West Germany. He was only seventeen. The other four stayed on for a short while and returned to England in December.

Four months in Hamburg had wrought noticeable changes on the young men from Liverpool. They had been thrown in at the deep end, experienced a stimulating, if disenchanting lifestyle, and grown old beyond their years. The long hours of playing had improved their technical skill immeasurably. Their style was now distinctive although as yet they were still not playing their own material, and their stage presence was forceful enough to quell the rowdiest of audiences. Back in Liverpool the fans were fast to notice the change and their shows had a riveting effect – especially on the girls. Pete Best,

the drummer, with his brooding, sensuous good looks, seemed to be the main attraction.

The Cavern Club used to be situated at 10 Matthew Street, Liverpool, down a flight of eighteen steps, beneath a warehouse. It was not exactly glamorous; the stage, seating and dance floor occupying three damp, interconnecting, tunnel-like cellars. In the neighbouring cellar was stored cheese whose smell, mingling with mould, beer and hot bodies, instilled a unique, if not instantly appealing aroma

Paul and his wife Linda are seen above *arriving for the Première, in London, of the James Bond film,* Live and Let Die *on June 6th 1973. Paul wrote the title song.*

to the club. Its owner, Ray McFall had hit on the brilliant, money-spinning notion to open the club at lunchtimes. These lunchtime sessions featured both jazz and beat groups, and a compère called Bob Wooler who was instrumental in bringing the Beatles to the Cavern Club. They made their début there on March 21st 1961 at a

Paul McCartney is seen left on his farm near Rye, Sussex, on January 28th 1980. This was his first day of freedom following nine days in prison in Japan, from where he was deported. He had been arrested at Tokyo Airport after arriving with his group Wings, for a concert tour. His offence was taking drugs into the country.

phrase, which introduced each of these hectic sessions was "Hi all you Cavern-dwellers – welcome to the best of cellars".

On November 9th 1961 Brian Epstein visited the Cavern Club, his curiosity roused by several enquiries concerning a record called My Bonnie by the Beatles. He was very excited by what he saw and heard. Several visits later Brian offered to manage the Beatles...and they accepted his offer. A contract was drafted, and signed, entitling him to twenty-five percent of future profits.

John Lennon, wearing a badge which says "I Still Love The Beatles", is pictured left with his psychedelic Rolls Royce. When the car was first shown, it met with cries of outrage that anyone should "deface" such a car, but it was the forerunner of many similarly attired vehicles.

Above: John dressed as a public lavatory commissionaire for a TV show in 1966.
Left: Relaxing in India, 1968.

fee of twenty-five shillings (£1.25) each.

Three days later they were back in Hamburg, with a booking at the Top Ten. George was now safely eighteen. Stu, reunited with his fiancée Astrid, decided to enrol at Hamburg State Art College, and gradually drifted away from the Beatles. Paul McCartney replaced him on bass guitar, and in June they cut a record as a backing group to Tony Sheridan, singing My Bonnie, for the Polydor label. On July 13th 1961, John, Paul, George and Pete returned to Liverpool, leaving Stu in Hamburg. Nine months later he died of a brain haemorrhage.

That summer had seen the launch, by one of John's former flatmates, of Mersey Beat, a fortnightly music newspaper. It was sold at newsagents, music shops and record counters in larger stores. One of these counters was in an electrical shop called NEMS. Run by the owner's son, Brian Epstein, it had a reputation as being

"the Finest Record Selection in the North".

Since returning from Hamburg, the Beatles had become regular performers at the Cavern Club. The reputation of the lunchtime sessions grew – as did the midday queues of office and shop girls. Loud music, long hair and anti-establishment image distinguished the Beatles from other local groups, and they invariably played to packed audiences enduring indescribable heat. The compère's catch-

Brian Epstein's first step was to try and win a recording contract. This proved to be more difficult than he had expected, but after many auditions and rejections, they were finally taken on, in the summer of 1962, by George Martin of EMI's Parlophone label. The only reservation expressed by George Martin concerned the drummer, Pete Best. He decided that he would replace him, for studio record-ings, with his own drummer. The Beatles went one better than George Martin, and replaced Pete altogether, with a drummer well remembered, and liked, from their Hamburg escapades – Richard Starkey, or Ringo Starr as he preferred to be known.

On August 23rd John Lennon married Cynthia Powell. She was expecting a baby. That same day Mersey Beat announced the sacking of Pete Best. The outcry at this

WAR
IS
OVER!

IF YOU WANT IT

Happy Christmas from John & Yoko

GIVE PEACE A CHANCE

Shortly before Christmas 1969, John and Yoko Ono-Lennon printed their Christmas peace message left. *Their "Peace Campaign" had begun earlier that year when, in March, they spent their honeymoon in public, sitting in bed surrounded by slogans.*

The "Peace Campaign" was publicised by the public honeymoon, or "bed-in", by sitting in a bag top left *known as "bagism", and by John sending back his M.B.E.*

John, Yoko and Kyoko — her daughter by a previous marriage, are seen right *in May 1969, at London Airport, on their way to the Bahamas where they staged another "bed-in".*

news was astonishing: petitions were signed, scuffles broke out, performances were disrupted; the girls had lost their handsome idol. It wasn't much fun for Ringo either.

Nevertheless, Ringo did fit in — both for his drumming skill, and his personality. The Beatles, locally at any rate, were extremely successful. A lot of girls were obsessively fanatical, literally fighting to

FROM ME TO YOU

be first through the doors and to the front row. Hints of what was to become the notorious "Beatlemania" were already evident – the girls used to scream as their heroes came on. One of the fans, Maureen Cox, later became Ringo's wife.

On September 4th 1962, the Beatles arrived at an elegant house in North London, EMI's recording studios. George

The Beatles in action these pages *are shown both in private, in the recording studio, and in public, where the all-important Beatle image was maintained to perfection. Their hair was washed every day, their shoes polished to mirror-brightness, and their smart, matching suits always pressed.*

PS I LOVE YOU

Martin had not been informed of the change in line-up, and consequently had his own drummer, Andy White, ready and waiting to play. They were shown round the studio. Its technicalities were explained to them, its versatility emphasised and the recording procedure outlined. Of the material presented to him, George Martin decided to record two Lennon-McCartney songs: the "A" side was *Love Me Do* and the "B" side *PS I Love You*. Some recordings were made using Andy White, with Ringo on tambourine or maracas, and others with Ringo in his proper role as drummer. At long last, after numerous takes, they were satisfied.

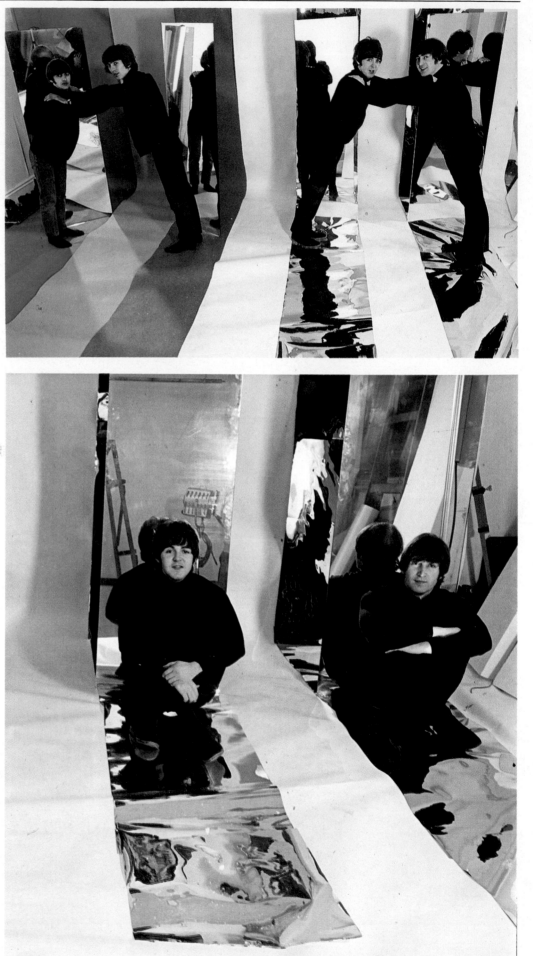

The Beatles went back to Liverpool to wait impatiently for the release, and hopefully the impact, of their record. It was released on October 5th 1962. The impact was not exactly earth-shattering. The singles chart was dominated by Americans including Ray Charles, Del Shannon and Carole King, whilst British singers like Kathy Kirby and Helen Shapiro enjoyed continuing success. However, their Liverpool fans bought the record in large numbers and wrote hundreds of letters to radio stations requesting it to be played. George said he "went shivery all over" when he first heard it on the airwaves. On October 27th *Love Me Do* entered the *Melody Maker* charts at Number 48. Brian Epstein had bought 10,000 copies. Two months later it reached Number 17 – the Beatles had a Top Twenty hit.

Rather than opting for one of the large, wealthy organisations, they decided to go for someone who really needed the money. George Martin suggested Dick James, who had once been a singer for Parlophone himself, his most successful recording being the theme song for the television series "Robin Hood". Dick James listened to, and quite liked *Love Me Do*, but felt that the Beatles' next recording should be something written by an outside songwriter. He came up with *How Do You Do It?* by Mitch Murray. George Martin liked it. The Beatles didn't.

"...without them the sixties and the whole of popular music would have been different."
Tony Palmer: All You Need Is Love.

John Winston Lennon (b.9-10-1940), James Paul McCartney (b.18-6-1942), George Harrison (b.25-2-1943) and Richard Starkey (b.7-7-1940) were the group to whom this accolade refers. By 1963, the ball had started rolling.

George Martin and Brian Epstein watched the chart progress of *Love Me Do* as keenly as their protégés. Its relative success, considering its lack of front-line publicity, was enough to stimulate a cautious optimism – it looked as though they had backed a winner.

The next move was to find a music publisher who would plug the songs.

On November 26th 1962 the Beatles were back in the studios to record their second single. George Martin played them a tape of *How Do You Do It?* and met with an obstinate lack of enthusiasm. They wanted to record one of their own songs. At George Martin's insistence they reluctantly produced a version of the song he wanted, and then, with great vivacity and enthusiasm, they played the Lennon-McCartney composition *Please Please Me*. George Martin, relenting, recorded it for release, and at the end of the session said "Gentlemen, you have just made your first Number One".

On December 17th the Beatles returned to Hamburg for a booking at the Star Club. They were not at all keen to go, but a contract is a contract and this one had been agreed before they had recorded anything. They were angry at the thought that they may be missing out on the opportunity to publicise *Love Me Do*, and to make matters worse, they were not even top of the bill! Their lack of enthusiasm showed in their playing during that two-week stint at the Star Club.

CAN'T BUY ME LOVE

The new year, 1963, saw them on tour in Scotland with one record in the charts and another soon to be released. *Please Please Me* was released on January 11th. The Beatles had made one television appearance, for Granada, in the North of England, back in October, but their nationwide début was to take place on January 19th, during a Saturday night pop music show called Thank Your Lucky Stars. Each act sang against an appropriate backdrop, and the Beatles were to

Opposite page: The Beatles in blazers and boaters rehearsing for a TV appearance with comedians Morecambe and Wise, broadcast in April 1964. The picture right was taken in Raymond's Revue Bar, London, in 1967, during the filming of a strip-tease scene which appeared in the film Magical Mystery Tour. *The Beatles give a Press conference below at the London home of their manager, Brian Epstein on May 19th 1967, announcing the release of* Sgt. Pepper's Lonely Hearts Club Band. *Bottom: A scene from the 1967 "Our World" TV spectacular. Below right: George Harrison, pavement artist; below far right: John waters a flower!*

be no exception—each member of the group was seen framed by a large heart. Brian Epstein had worked his own magic on their image; instead of the aggressive leather gear of the Hamburg days, they had clean, brushed-forward hair, clean-shaven faces, smart suits and cheerful smiles. Their sound and presentation prompted Brian Matthew, the show's compère, to rate the Beatles as "...musically and visually the most

accomplished group to emerge since the Shadows".

The national newspapers still had not expressed any interest in the Beatles, apart from the *Evening Standard* which ran a feature in February. Maureen Cleave's piece encapsulated the four thus: "John Lennon has an upper lip which is brutal in a devastating way. George Harrison is handsome, whimsical and untidy. Paul McCartney has a round baby face while

These and the following pages illustrate one of the Beatles' phenomenally successful tours of America. The tour in the summer of 1964 lasted 32 days during which they travelled 22,441 miles, visited 24 cities in the United States and Canada, and gave 31 performances.

As far as Britain was concerned, the Beatles' visit to the United States was a tremendous diplomatic success. Britain's prime minister, Sir Alec Douglas-Home, returning from America, said of the Beatles "They are my secret weapon".

Ringo Starr is ugly but cute.''

On February 2nd, the Beatles embarked on their first nationwide tour. Its promoter was Arthur Howes, and Helen Shapiro, the schoolgirl star was topping the bill. They were to play in theatres all over the country. At the beginning of the tour, *Please Please Me* had started to climb the charts but audience response to the Beatles was not wildly enthusiastic. On February 16th, the record had reached

Number Two and the Beatles were called back to reappear on Thank Your Lucky Stars and a couple of radio programmes. The response from the fans was improving.

When *Melody Maker*'s charts showed the Beatles at Number One on March 2nd, Liverpool went wild. Arthur Howes sent them on another tour, this time supporting two American stars, Chris Montez and Tommy Roe. It soon became clear from audience reaction that the order should be

changed – the Beatles were moved to top of the bill, finishing each night with the Isley Brothers' classic, *Twist and Shout*.

Brian Epstein was delighted. George Martin decided that it was time to make an LP. The LP with the title of the single, *Please Please Me,* was released on March 22nd 1963. All the tracks were numbers that George Martin had heard them do at the Cavern Club, and all were recorded in one twelve-hour session, finishing with *Twist and Shout* exuberantly yelled by John Lennon. What seemed to surprise the reviewers was that this was not yet another LP full of rubbish cashing in on a hit single. It proved beyond doubt that the Beatles were songwriters.

Cliff Richard's *Summer Holiday* ousted *Please Please Me* from the Number One slot after a couple of weeks. Then, on the day that the LP was released, March 22nd, Gerry and the Pacemakers, also Epstein/Martin protégés, reached Number One with the song that the Beatles had turned down – *How Do You Do It?*

On April 12th *From Me To You*, their third single, was released amidst a fanfare of publicity, but unenthusiastic reviews. Nevertheless it reached Number One on April 27th. Gerry and the Pacemakers were still at Number Three, and another Beatles' composition, *Do You Want To*

Know a Secret? sung by Billy J Kramer, was also riding high. To cap it all, the *Please Please Me* LP had reached the top of the *Melody Maker* charts.

Meanwhile, on April 8th, John Lennon's wife, a well kept secret as far as the fans were concerned, had given birth to a baby boy – Julian.

NEMS Enterprises now had a Liverpool office and Beatles' Fan Club, and a London office housing the southern region fan club and publicity man, Tony Barrow, who had once worked for Decca. Nationwide newsletters were published

regularly, the Beatles working very closely with the club. Every Christmas from 1963 to 1969 they recorded a message especially for the fans, and not for commercial sale. Applications for membership ran into tens of thousands, and the offices were inundated with cards, gifts and assorted toys.

Topping the bill officially for the first time, on tour with Roy Orbison, the screaming began. At every venue the fans went wild and by the end of each perform-

ance the stage was littered with jelly babies, because somewhere George Harrison had mentioned that he liked them.

Following a concert in The Royal Albert Hall, London, Paul McCartney met, and was instantly attracted to Jane Asher. Her mother was a professional musician, and her father, Sir Richard Asher, a well-known psychiatrist. From then, until the end of 1966, Paul lived with Jane and her parents whenever he was in London.

That summer, every concert was a sell-out. They played at the Cavern Club for the 292nd and last time on August 3rd, and on August 23rd, *She Loves You* was released. It was to remain in the charts for the next twenty-four weeks.

On September 11th, the Beatles were

Every concert that the Beatles performed was characterised by a deafening scream from the audience, and the term "Beatlemania" was coined to imply Beatle-related hysteria. It did not seem to matter what they played – their presence on stage was enough!

top of *Melody Maker*'s popularity poll, and the *Mirror* ran a two page story on them. At last the national newspapers were really taking notice.

"Beatlemania" was born on the night of October 13th, the event surrounded by mystery. Beatle fans had screamed at concerts and pestered their relatives back home; the fan club had grown to vast proportions, and every record was a success; but nothing quite like the unprecedented scenes described in Monday's newspapers, had ever happened before.

Emerging from a performance on "Sunday Night at The London Palladium", hosted by compère Bruce Forsyth, the Beatles were said to have been greeted by hordes of shrieking teenagers, restrained not entirely successfully by a long-suffering police force. The newspaper photographs, which appeared with the story, were close-up shots with four or five fans and a couple of policemen filling the frame. One witness said that there were no more than eight girls outside the theatre.

Two days before, *She Loves You* had sold over a million copies and become their first "Gold Disc". The song's repeated "Yeah! Yeah! Yeah!" became part of the legend.

Although the origins of Beatlemania may have been puzzling, there was no denying its existence. The Beatles' meteoric rise to fame had resulted in an extraordinary phenomenon, which was to last for three years and cover most of the world. The girls literally screamed, wept, hurled themselves at the stage...some were so hysterical that they actually foamed at the mouth, wet themselves and fainted. It was terrifying.

This must have been a difficult time for the four Liverpool lads who, for all their success, regarded themselves primarily as musicians – for not only was the audience

ANOTHER DAY

row so deafening that they could not have heard a note even if they wanted to, but all that the newspapers seemed to mention was the hysteria. As far as the concerts were concerned, the music did not matter any more.

The media conspired to popularise the Beatles, not only with teenagers, many of whom had started to grow their hair, but also with a wider audience. Four such charming, clean (they washed their hair *every* day), witty boys could not possibly pose a threat. Respectability was guaranteed when Buckingham Palace

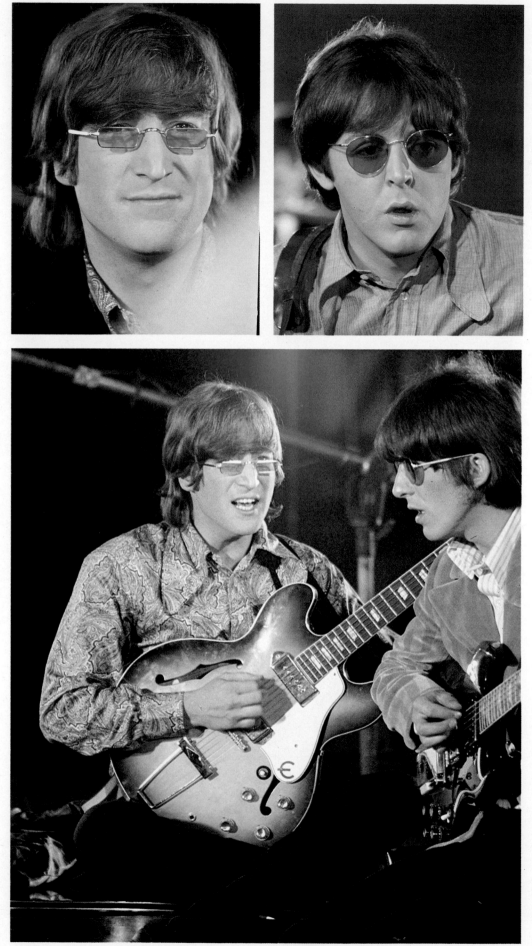

approved their inclusion in the Royal Command Variety Performance to be held on November 4th. In the meantime they were to play their first foreign tour, in Sweden from October 24th to 29th.

Excited Swedish fans greeted the Beatles wherever they went; imitating their clothes and hairstyle, known there as the "Hamlet Cut", and screaming just as loudly as the British fans. The Beatles themselves dated the true eruption of Beatlemania to the extraordinary day that

GIRL

August 15th 1965: Overleaf and the following sequence *are taken from the film of the Beatles' appearance at the Shea Stadium* where they played to about 60,000 fans. The Beatles considered this concert to be the pinnacle of their touring career. A contemporary report said: "Never before in the world of show business has there been an audience to equal the numbers that filled the vast Shea Stadium in New York – 60,000 plus poured into the huge arena: boys, girls – young and not so young – to get their fill of *BEATLES*. Before actually appearing...the boys decided to get a bird's eye view of the place and the best way to do that was to hire a helicopter... But even this formidable sight did not subdue their infectious high spirits."

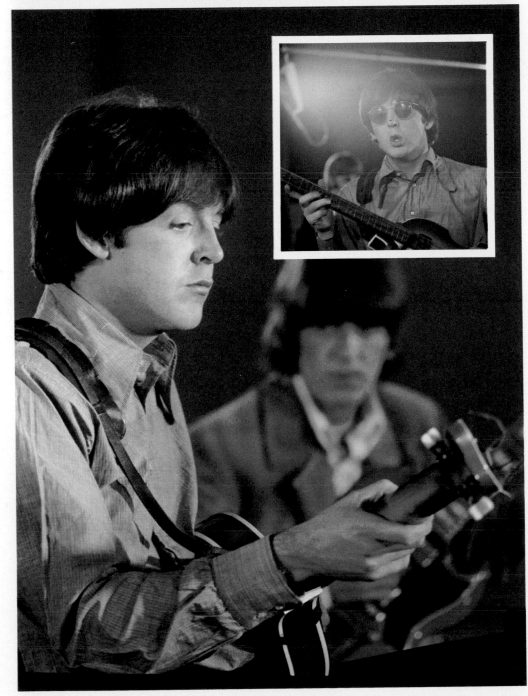

they returned from Sweden. London's Heathrow Airport had never seen anything like it. Hours before the Beatles were due to land, crowds had started arriving to greet their returning heroes, and as the aircraft landed, everyone started yelling. Suddenly they themselves realised just how popular they had become.

The Queen Mother and Princess Margaret were the Royal representatives who attended the Royal Command Variety Performance at the Prince of Wales Theatre, London, on the evening of November 4th 1963. They were greeted by

IT'S ONLY LOVE

HELLO...

a cheering crowd, Beatle fans mingling with those who had come to look at the "Royals". The evening was a great success, the Beatles performing their most popular songs – introducing *Twist and Shout* with the request that those "... in the cheap seats clap their hands...the rest of you just rattle your jewellery". The Press were ecstatic, the *Daily Mirror* heading its article "Yeah! Yeah! Yeah!" and continuing "... You'd have to be a real sour square not to love the nutty, noisy, happy, handsome Beatles."

A Beatle industry was beginning to grow as various businesses, scenting large profits, jumped on the band-wagon. Beatle-inspired products started to go on sale; pullovers, collarless jackets and wigs being among the first. The media, also cashing in, called upon psychiatrists to analyse Beatlemania. One pinpointed the hysterics as "...relieving a sexual urge", and the *News of the World* suggested "...the girls are preparing for motherhood. Their frenzied screams are a rehearsal for that moment...even the jelly

them down. Finally Brian Epstein paid Capitol a visit, and persuaded them to release *I Want To Hold Your Hand*. A date was set: January 13th 1964. He also met Ed Sullivan whose talent-spotting television show was renowned across the continent for helping new acts succeed. Brian insisted on the Beatles getting top billing, and managed to get away with it. They were booked to play two shows on 9th and 16th February.

The Beatles' winter tour of Britain, though the fans would never know it, was a nightmare. Their success had reached terrifying proportions, and they needed guarding constantly. To escape the mobs they had to rush off stage and out to a waiting vehicle, shivering in wet stage suits. They even needed someone to screen the Press, that job falling to Brian Sommerville, their PR man.

That winter saw merchandise as diverse as "signed" guitars and aprons, lockets

babies are symbolic.''

Four dramatically photographed black and white faces adorned the cover of *With The Beatles*. This was their second LP. It had been recorded in July and was released, to advance orders of a quarter of a million, on November 22nd 1963. The same day, the President of the United States, John F Kennedy, was shot dead.

The Beatles' Christmas release was *I Want To Hold Your Hand*. Advance orders of one million copies made it an instant Number One.

Brian Epstein and George Martin decided that it was time to conquer America. *Please Please Me, From Me To You* and *She Loves You* had all been released there but met with indifference. EMI's American Capitol label had turned

NORWEGIAN WOOD

and boots, wigs and clothes. Vast quantities of manufactured goods came into the shops just in time for Christmas. Brian Epstein delegated the responsibility for dealing with copyright infringements, and issuing new licences, to his London solicitors, who in turn passed it on to a third party. Two Companies were formed, Stramsact and Seltaeb. Seltaeb (Beatles spelt backwards) would deal with American licences should the need arise. A ludicrous deal was agreed upon entitling Stramsact-Seltaeb to ninety percent and NEMS Enterprises to ten percent of any profits.

Before their United States visit, the Beatles had a booking to play in Paris. They discovered the French audiences and Press to be indifferent. This disappointment evaporated into thin air when some remarkable news arrived: *I Want To Hold Your Hand* had shot up to Number One in America. The Beatles were stunned. "They just sat on the floor like kittens at Brian's feet", said photographer, Dezo Hoffman.

American reporters arrived in force to interview the Beatles, and to coincide with all this publicity, fifty thousand dollars were spent on promoting their visit to the United States. A concert at the Washington Coliseum, and two at the Carnegie Hall were sold out, whilst the Ed Sullivan show was inundated with requests for studio tickets. Suddenly, all the American radio stations were playing Beatles records. Their LPs, *Please Please Me* and *With The Beatles* (released in America as *Meet The Beatles*), and various singles were all high in the American charts. Cashing in on their success was Seltaeb,

RUN FOR YOUR LIFE

The Beatles did not confine their talents solely to music – films these pages – were another outlet for their creativity. Above is a scene from a 1967 movie called How I Won The War, *in which John Lennon plays a soldier, Private Gripweed (3rd from left). For the part he had to cut his hair and wear his glasses, and after filming he decided to keep this image for his real-life role.*

busily negotiating lucrative merchandising deals.

Any nerves that the Beatles may have felt during their flight to America on February 7th 1964, were dispelled at the sight of Kennedy Airport as they landed. Thousands – reports vary between three and ten thousand – of screaming youngsters chanting "We love you Beatles, Oh yes we do..." were there to greet them.

Two days later, their appearance on the Ed Sullivan Show was watched by 73 million television viewers. Throughout America, statistics showed the lowest teenage crime rate for fifty years!

On February 11th the Beatles appeared on the revolving stage of the Washington Coliseum. Having been bombarded by jelly beans from all sides, George complained "They don't have soft jelly babies in America, but hard jelly beans like bullets". They hurt.

The following day, the Beatles performed two triumphant concerts at Carnegie Hall, to uproarious crowds of six

thousand. They then flew to Miami for their second Ed Sullivan Show. The broadcast broke all previous viewing records.

On February 25th George Harrison celebrated his twenty-first birthday, and at the beginning of March the Beatles returned to England and the now familiar airport hysteria.

They started work on their first film, *A Hard Day's Night*, in the first week of March. One of the members of the cast

was a model called Pattie Boyd. She and George Harrison started going out together and eventually she moved into his house in Esher, Surrey. They married a year later.

Can't Buy Me Love, the Beatles' sixth single, was released on March 20th in Britain and America to advance orders of three million copies. Three days later John Lennon's book, *In His Own Write*, came out, and almost predictably flew to the top of the best-seller list. Ringo Starr was elected vice-president of Leeds University, England, and Madame Tussaud's Wax Museum in London included models of the Beatles in its display.

That summer, they toured Europe, Hong Kong, New Zealand and Australia where they were greeted by their biggest crowd ever: in Adelaide 300,000 turned out to greet them.

A Hard Day's Night had its Royal Première in July, closely followed by the LP of the same name.

Thirty-two days of gruelling touring began on August 19th 1964. During this American tour, the Beatles performed in twenty-four cities in America and Canada. They travelled 22,441 miles, sixty hours of which were by air. Those days seemed to be an endless round of concerts, Press conferences, schedules, hotels... after a night in one of those hotels, an enterprising businessman cut their pillowslips into 160,000 little squares, mounted them on certificates, and sold them for a dollar each.

That year, the world was their oyster, but it was out of their reach. If the world had to be locked out, then they had to be locked in. At one airport they were taken straight from the aircraft into a protective iron cage – a necessary precaution against being crushed to death! Beatlemania was not only evident during live appearances, but also in cinemas, where showings of *A Hard Day's Night* were invariably accompanied by screaming audiences. The songs on the LP reflected their life on the run.

In October 1964, Britain's Conservative

Overleaf *is shown one of the many spectacular scenes which make up the film* Magical Mystery Tour. *The Beatles produced, directed and starred in the 60-minute extravaganza, edited from hundreds of hours of film footage. Despite the fact that the film was a product of the charismatic Beatles, the critics were unimpressed, and the Beatles were hurt by its unenthusiastic reception.*

MICHELLE

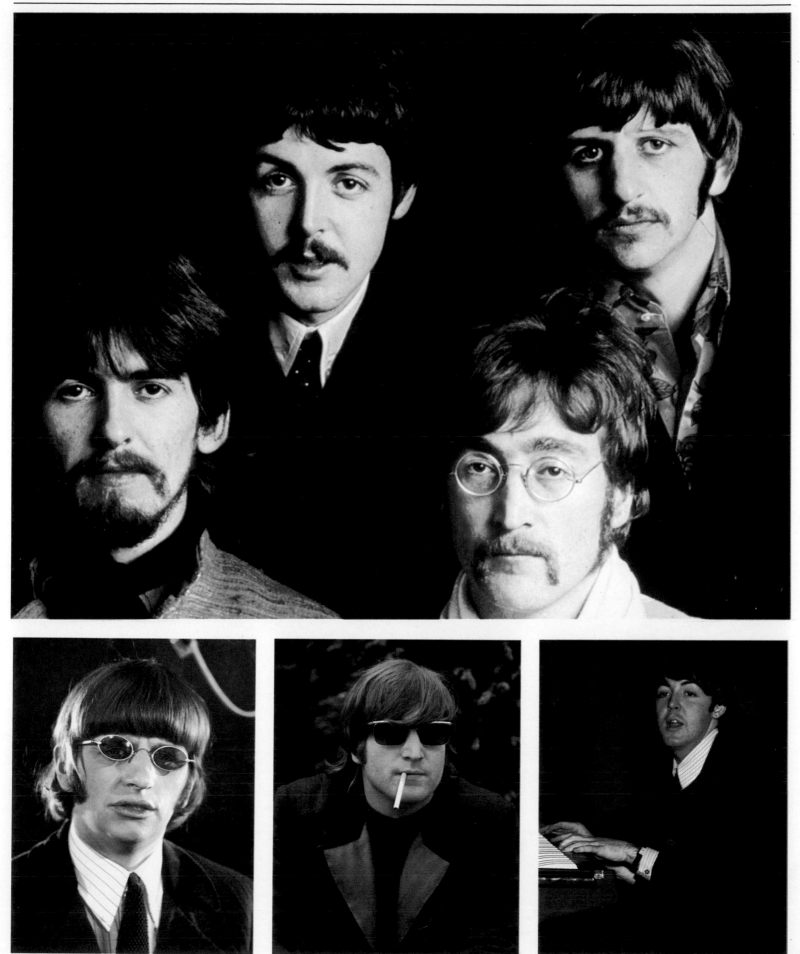

ALL YOU NEED IS LOVE

government of thirteen years, was defeated by the Labour party under Harold Wilson. He was a shrewd politician who realised the advantages in being the pop world's friend. The Beatles provided a superb opportunity for self glorification. He included them in the Honours List for 1965. They were awarded Membership of the Most Excellent Order of the British Empire, or the M.B.E. The Beatles' reactions were mixed. John thought "…you had to drive tanks and win wars to get the M.B.E.", and George "…didn't

On June 25th 1967, a six-hour TV programme called "Our World" was broadcast, via satellite, to many nations. Estimates suggest that some 200 million people saw the event, during which the Beatles performed, and recorded, a song written especially for the occasion, All You Need Is Love, this page.

think you got that sort of thing just for playing Rock and Roll". On a more frivolous note, Paul asked "What does that make my Dad?", and Ringo said he would "…keep it to dust when I'm old".

On December 4th their fourth LP, *Beatles For Sale*, was released. The Beatles' success was, of course, reflected in their wealth. They bought luxury cars and houses and gifts for themselves and their relatives. They smoked marijuana and tried pills with such exotic names as **Purple Hearts** and **Yellow Submarines**. Lysergic Acid Diethylamide, or LSD, was not yet illegal. Its hallucinogenic properties seemed to epitomise the mid nineteen sixties.

1965 has been variously hailed as the year of Swinging London and Carnaby Street, short skirts and flowery shirts, floppy hats and frivolity. The Beatles, with their music, hair style and clothes, set the precedent.

Their most important tour that year was their third visit to America which took place during the last two weeks in August. The triumph of that tour took place in the New York Mets' baseball ground, the Shea Stadium. The Beatles played to a screaming crowd of 56,000.

That month, *Help!*, their fifth album, was brought out. One of the songs on it, *Yesterday,* has since been recorded, by different artists, about 2,000 times. The film *Help!*, made earlier that year, was a surrealist adventure starring Ringo, and

Overleaf *are some scenes from the sequence of film which was shot for TV to accompany broadcasts, in the UK, of the song* Penny Lane, *released in 1967. The record in fact had two "A" sides: on the other was* Strawberry Fields Forever.

STRAWBERRY FIELDS FOREVER

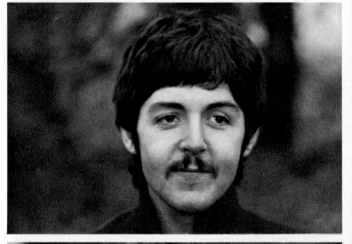

LADY MADONNA

"...more popular than Jesus now". Just before their arrival in America, news of this "blasphemous" remark was spread across the continent on the cover of a teenage magazine called *Datebook*.

In Nashville, Tennessee, Beatles records were ceremoniously burnt in public bonfires, setting a precedent in the American South. Threatening letters and telephone calls to the Beatles frightened them. Their fear of being crushed to death by an adoring crowd was displaced by fear of assassination on that vulnerable stage. When

The trappings of wealth included mansion-like houses, and John, George and Ringo all opted for stockbroker-belt Surrey these pages. Paul lived in London.

filmed in England, Austria and the Bahamas.

Rubber Soul, the title a pun on white artists playing soul music, was released on December 3rd. The album's significance lay in its sophistication. The lyrics were comments on their own lives, and on subjects that mattered to them. The songs were recorded over weeks rather than hours, and consisted of complex, superimposed sounds. One track was laid over another in EMI's recording studio, under George Martin's guiding hand.

The rounds of concerts and tours continued, and ended bitterly and sadly in the summer of 1966, in America. Several months before the tour, in an interview in London's *Evening Standard*, John had said in passing, that the Beatles were

BABY YOU'RE A RICH MAN

they arrived in America, John publicly apologised for his remark at a Press conference.

The last concert of the tour was on August 29th in San Francisco's Candlestick Park. It was also their last concert. By the time they finished touring, they all hated it. George said the touring "...was great at first...But it got played out. We got in a rut." The end of touring was the end of Beatlemania and the end of an era.

Towards the end of that long, hot, hazy summer, the Beatles released an LP called *Revolver*. This, their seventh album, seemed somehow to reflect the Beatles as individuals. Ringo was the happy writer of *Yellow Submarine*, whilst George's bitter *Taxman,* Paul's gentle *Here There And Everywhere*, and John's enigmatic *Tomorrow Never Knows* all echoed something in their respective characters. This individualism was reflected in their appearance which no longer bore the stamp of uniformity associated with their stage act. John had cut his hair short and now wore little round-framed glasses. He took the hallucinogenic drug LSD. George also experimented with LSD, and had become interested in Indian religion. He was learning to play the sitar under the expert tuition of Ravi Shankar. Ringo, the family man, spent most of his time with his wife Maureen and their baby son Zak, whilst Paul and Jane Asher were firmly ensconced in Paul's London house, situated

near EMI's recording studios. Brian Epstein's role had diminished considerably in importance.

At the beginning of 1967 the Beatles released a brilliant single. It had two "A" sides. On one was Paul's delightful cameo of an area of Liverpool remembered from childhood, *Penny Lane*, whilst on the other, *Strawberry Fields Forever* was John's dreamy, drug-influenced recollection of a Salvation Army home near where he'd grown up.

Sergeant Pepper's Lonely Hearts Club Band is seen by many people to be the Beatles' masterpiece. It was met with

soaring critical acclaim, *The Times Literary Supplement* hailing the Beatles as "a barometer of our times". The lyrics are incredibly vivid, and range from the psychedelic *Lucy In The Sky With Diamonds*, initials LSD, to the gentle sentiments expressed in *When I'm Sixty-Four*. The final track, entitled *A Day In The Life*, stunned everyone who heard it, its climax being a hysterical, illogical barrage of noise. Its very last note is so high-pitched that it is only audible to dogs!

Reactions to this, their eighth album, varied. References to drugs, whether intended or not, resulted in intensive studies of the words which were printed on

the sleeve, both by Beatle-worshipping drug-takers and panic-stricken establishment figures. At one end of the scale, the Beatles were hailed as prophets and at the other, viewed with fear and repulsion. The BBC banned *A Day In The Life*. John became so sick of the rumpus that he started denying that any deliberate references had been made to drugs at all.

June 1967 was an eventful month for the Beatles. Not only had they released their "masterpiece", but they were also Britain's contribution to an event, planned by many nations for the advocation of international peace. The programme, relayed by satellite, was watched by 200 million people. The Beatles' largest

Sgt. Pepper's Lonely Hearts Club Band is seen by many to represent the peak of the Beatles' musical career, and to have revolutionised popular music. The psychedelic colours of their costumes centre right *and* overleaf *reflect the vivid imagery found in the lyrics, and performances of the music cried out for a theatrical interpretation* these pages. *George Martin's role in the creation of the album, which took over 700 hours to record, cannot be overemphasised, especially as many of the techniques employed, which had never been used before, somehow became a reality – or a dream – under his guiding hand.*

audience saw them perform a song written especially for the occasion called *All You Need Is Love*. The programme was broad-

I AM THE WALRUS

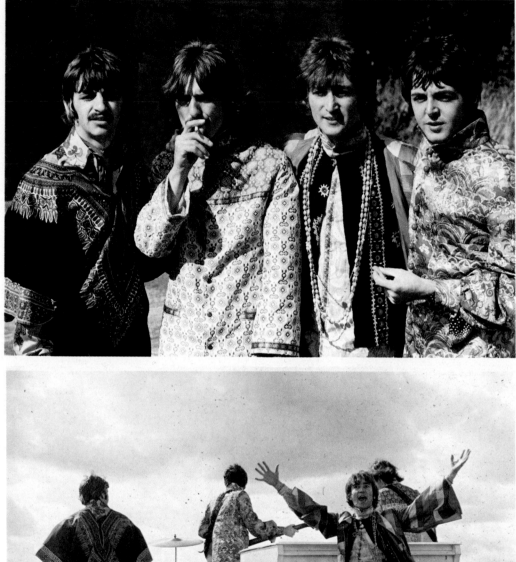

The same day, Brian Epstein set off for his mansion in Sussex, intending to spend the weekend in the country. But he found the peace and quiet of the country frustrating, and within a few hours he had returned to London. By this time he no longer tried to hide his homosexuality, and had even admitted to the Press that he had taken LSD. He relied heavily on drugs, long bouts of drug-induced hyper-activity followed by long hours of drug-induced sleep. On Sunday August 27th 1967, Brian Epstein did not wake up.

A telephone call to the Beatles in Wales told them that Brian was dead. The inquest's verdict was accidental overdose, although the newspapers suggested that he had committed suicide.

These pages *and* overleaf *show scenes from the film* Magical Mystery Tour. *Filming commenced on September 11th 1967 when the Beatles and various extras, including a hired fat lady, a midget and a music-hall funny man, boarded a decorated coach and set off for the south of England. Apart from random "on location" sequences shot wherever the scenery looked interesting, they also filmed in a disused airfield in Kent. The hundreds of hours of film took 11 weeks to edit!*

cast two weeks after the Arab-Israeli Six Day War.

For many people *All You Need Is Love*, with its repetitive, almost hypnotic chorus, encapsulates the sweetly scented, long-haired, idealistic summer of '67. In August the Beatles went to a seminar given by the Maharishi Mahesh Yogi and heard him speak of sublime consciousness and inner peace, and what he said struck a sympathetic chord. The following day they went with him to Wales, curious to learn more.

In September 1967, a bunch of assorted actors and extras boarded a hired coach with the Beatles, to film *The Magical Mystery Tour*. The end result was a series of disconnected scenes and events, lacking any satisfactory organisation. The Press saw it as their "First Official Failure".

In November their next single, *Hello Goodbye*, was released, and successfully reached Number One in both Britain and America. That Christmas also saw evidence of the Beatles' new venture, their own company—Apple Corps—"a pun" Paul said helpfully.

MAGICAL MYSTERY TOUR

Apple began with a boutique in Baker Street, conceived by Paul as "a beautiful place where you can buy beautiful things". Upstairs from the boutique were Apple's offices, housing the Beatles' own recording and publishing company, where they could be free from John's detested "men in suits" normally associated with business. The general idea was that business should be fun, and run by peace-loving, unselfish, gentle young people.

Apple had only been in operation for a few months when the Maharishi Mahesh Yogi welcomed the Beatles to Rishikesh, India, in February 1968. They had arrived for a three-month course of religious studies. Within ten days, Ringo and his wife Maureen had gone home. The others fasted, chanted and prayed, meditated and wrote songs. But they returned to England disillusioned and bored. They were also bored with playing shopkeepers, and the Apple boutique, from which more had been stolen than bought, was closed down.

That May, a friendship that had been growing between John Lennon and Yoko

Ono, became something more special. He had first met her in 1966 at one of her London art exhibitions where, instead of giving him a business card, she had handed him a card with the word "breathe" printed on it.

Coinciding with the start of John's new relationship was the unhappy break-up of Paul's five year liaison with Jane Asher. They had been engaged for six months. Paul said that the break-up was the source of inspiration for the Beatles' next, and most successful single, *Hey Jude*. It was their first Apple record, and its playing time was just over seven minutes.

The Beatles and cast of the Magical Mystery Tour *stop at a fish-and-chip shop for lunch* above.
Opposite: *Promotional film clip for the 1966 single,* Paperback Writer.

By this time, Apple had moved to a very elegant house in London's prestigious Savile Row. The Beatles' first LP on Apple records was a double album. Simply called *The Beatles* it was startlingly simply clothed in a white cover. Opinions on this album vary considerably. Some critics lavished praise upon it, whilst others saw clear rifts between the four Beatles illustrated in its songs. Paul's sweet ballad style had not been subjected to John's cynicism, and John's aggression had not been tempered by Paul's harmony.

The Beatles was released on November 22nd 1968. The previous day, Yoko Ono had had a miscarriage and two weeks before that, John and Cynthia Lennon had been granted a divorce. On November 28th, John was fined for possessing cannabis, and the following day, *Two*

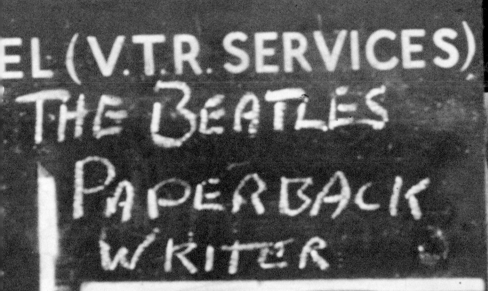

EL (V.T.R. SERVICES)

THE BEATLES

PAPERBACK

WRITER

1

Virgins, an avant-garde LP by John and Yoko was released. Its cover depicted the couple naked, and following public outrage, the LP was sold under more modest brown paper wrappings.

In the meantime, an American photographer, Linda Eastman, with Heather, her small daughter by a previous marriage, had moved in with Paul McCartney.

Apple Corps was proving to be a heavy

task, John announced that he had found someone better qualified to cope with the mess, a tough New York music manager called Allen Klein. Eventually, a three-to-one vote established Allen Klein as manager, Paul bitterly clinging to his choice, the Eastmans. It was the beginning of a power struggle which resulted in an unpleasant shadow greying their last months together as Beatles.

financial burden. Although the record division was very successful, estimates suggest that Apple was losing around £20,000 each week through poor investments, lavish staff expenditure and myriad hangers-on. The unselfish, gentle young people were just as greedy and grabbing as anyone else. The Beatles decided that experienced outsiders would have to tackle the task of sorting out Apple's finances.

A New York law firm called Eastman and Eastman, Paul's future in-laws, were approached. A few weeks after the Eastmans had embarked on their colossal

A sea-shore location for one of Magical Mystery Tour*'s sequences is shown* these pages. *The colour film was scheduled for viewing in Britain on Boxing Day 1967. 15 million people watched the broadcast – most on black and white TVs – and many were dismayed and puzzled by what they saw: one critic went so far as to call the film "blatant rubbish"!*

In January 1969, in the basement of the Apple building, the Beatles recorded a group of songs which would not be released until May 1970. The project involved a documentary film and an album under the title, *Let It Be*. One episode of the film records the Beatles' last ever public appearance together, when they played on the roof of the Apple building on January 30th 1969.

On March 12th Paul McCartney and Linda Eastman married, and a crowd of weeping girls gathered miserably outside Paul's London house.

John Lennon and Yoko Ono married in Gibraltar on March 20th. Their honey-

HEY JUDE

moon, in full view of the world, outraged the Press. They spent a week sitting in bed in a hotel in Amsterdam, Holland, surrounded by slogans advocating peace. They called it a "Bed-in".

Their next public appearance occurred on April 1st. The two of them sat in a bag

Scenes from Magical Mystery Tour *these pages include John Lennon looking almost unrecognisable in a long beard. The film may not have been a critical success, but the soundtrack included several brilliant, and memorable songs such as* Fool On The Hill, Blue Jay Way, *and* I Am The Walrus.

on a table in a luxurious hotel in Vienna, Austria, and called it "Bagism". In May they staged another "Bed-in", this time in Montreal, Canada, which culminated in a bedside recording of a song entitled *Give Peace A Chance*. John and Yoko had started their "Peace campaign".

Abbey Road, the Beatles' best-selling LP, was the outcome of a longing to make just one more album the way they used to, with George Martin editing and producing the way he used to. This, their last recorded LP, was created at EMI's Abbey Road studios during July and August 1969. The return to the discipline and structure so evident in some of their earlier work, resulted in a highly polished, memorable album; one particular song, *Here Comes The Sun*, exuded such freshness and optimism that it seemed to look forward to the new decade.

The release of *Abbey Road* had one rather peculiar side effect. Its cover prompted a rumour that became almost a cult – that Paul McCartney was dead. The Beatles, simply crossing a road, were seen as a funeral procession. John, in white, was cast as the minister, George as the grave-digger in practical denim, and dark-suited Ringo the undertaker. Paul mean-

Overleaf: In February 1968, leaving their newly-born company, Apple Corps, far behind them, the Beatles travelled to Rishikesh, India, to meditate, relax and hopefully acquire spiritual and mental peace under the guidance of the Maharishi Mahesh Yogi. The main picture shows the Beatles, their wives, their road manager, Mal Evans (in glasses, second from the right), Mike Love of the Beach Boys (far right), and behind them, in front of his garlanded picture, the garlanded guru. The inset shows two more devotees, Mia Farrow (centre) and Donovan (in yellow). The relaxed Himalayan holiday camp atmosphere was not tempting enough for Ringo, and he and Maureen left after 10 days to get back to their children, Zak and Jason. The next to leave were Paul McCartney and Jane Asher. John and George persevered for a while longer but eventually they too came to realise that their guru was only human, and perhaps did not hold the mysterious key that they were searching for. Disillusioned, the Beatles cut all ties with the Maharishi.

In December 1980, the man who had tried to "Give Peace A Chance", met with his cruel and violent death. He was 40 years old. For many people John Lennon was much more than a musician, he was a spiritual leader, a guru. All over the world, people gathered to mourn together. Outside Moscow, on the Lenin Hills, a crowd gathered to pay tribute in a silent vigil. The stars on the American flag had been blacked out "because America couldn't keep the life of Lennon". In New York and in Liverpool, thousands gathered, and as the sun set, the candles flickered and they said goodbye.

while, walked barefooted, and out of step. A car numberplate in the background read "28 IF", or Paul's age IF he had lived. When confronted with this rumour, Paul's reply was, "I'm alive and well, but if I were dead I would be the last to know!"

As the sixties drew to a close, John Lennon returned his M.B.E. to the Queen. Apple had dwindled to a purely administrative office. The spring of the new decade saw the end of the Beatles.

Thousands of people hoped and prayed that the Beatles would reunite, if only for just one more concert. To one of the many requests, Paul commented simply, "You cannot reheat a soufflé". Nevertheless, as far as the world was concerned, there was always a chance, however tiny, that the four would rejoin in friendship and harmony one day. That chance was brutally shattered once and for all on December 8th 1980, when John Lennon was shot dead. The memories will linger and slowly fade, but the music is forever.

First English edition published in 1981 by Colour Library International Ltd.
This edition published by Crescent Books.
Distributed by Crown Publishers Inc.
Text ©: Colour Library International Ltd.
Illustrations ©: Keystone Press Agency Ltd, London, England.
h g f e d c b a
Colour separations by FERCROM, Barcelona, Spain.
Display and text filmsetting by Focus Photoset and The Printed Word,
London, England.
Printed and bound in Barcelona, Spain, by JISA-RIEUSSET and EUROBINDER.
Library of Congress Catalog Card No: 81-68731